OLYMPIC LIBRARY

Modern Olympics

Richard Tames

Heinemann

First published in Great Britain by Heinemann Publishers
(Oxford) Ltd
Halley Court, Jordan Hill, Oxford OX2 8EJ

MADRID ATHENS PARIS
FLORENCE PRAGUE WARSAW
PORTSMOUTH NH CHICAGO SAO PAULO
SINGAPORE TOKYO MELBOURNE AUCKLAND
IBADAN GABORONE JOHANNESBURG

Designed by VAP Group Ltd
Printed in the UK by Jarrold Printing, Norwich

00 99 98 97 96
10 9 8 7 6 5 4 3 2 1

ISBN 0 431 05941 1

British Library Cataloguing in Publication Data

Tames, Richard
  Modern Olympics. — (Olympic Library)
  I. Title II. Series
  796.48

Acknowledgements
The Publishers would like to thank the following for permission to reproduce photographs:
The Ronald Grant Archive: p.4; Hulton Deutsch: p.5; Colorsport/Barrett Collection: p.6; Mary Evans Picture Library: p.7;
Popperfoto: p.8, 9, 10; The Allsport Historical Collection: p.11; Allsport/Billy Stickland: p.12; Colorsport: p.13;
Presse-Sports: p.15; Mirrorpic: p.16; Hulton Deutsch: p.18, 19; Range/Bettman/UPI: p.20;
Allsport/Allsport/IOC: p.21, 22, 23, 24; Hulton Deutsch: p.25; The Ronald Grant Archive: p.26; Allsport/Dave Cannon:
p.27; Associated Sports Photography: p.28, 29.

Cover photographs reproduced with permission of Colorsport and Professional Sport.
Cover designed by Brigitte Willgoss.

Our thanks to Mr Robert Paul of the US Olympic Committee, Mr Stan Greenberg and Mr Paul Rowbotham for their
comments in the preparation of this book.

Olympic rings logo reproduced with the permission of the International Olympic Committee.

Every effort has been made to contact copyright holders of any material reproduced in this book.
Any omissions will be rectified in subsequent printings if notice is given to the Publisher.

Contents

The First Modern Olympics

A javelin thrower – a still from the film *Olympia* by Leni Riefenstahl.

The Ancient Olympics

For over a thousand years, from 776BC to AD393, Games were held every four years at Olympia in western Greece. The contests usually lasted for five days and drew male competitors from all over the Greek-speaking world. The events consisted of races for runners, chariots and horses, **javelin**, **discus** and bloody combat events. The prizes were olive wreaths – and immortal fame.

Reviving the Games

In the nineteenth century five nations led the way in reviving the idea of the ancient Olympics. British boarding schools stressed games as the best way of 'building character' in young people.

American colleges took competitive sport a stage further by developing programmes of training and coaching. French and German **archaeologists excavated** the swampy site of Olympia itself. The Greeks organized four 'Olympics' between 1859 and 1889 but only Greeks competed and almost no-one outside Greece knew about them. It was a Frenchman, Baron Pierre de Coubertin (1863–1937), who brought these interests together to organize the first true modern Olympics.

Father of the Olympics

Baron de Coubertin believed that sport could be the religion of the modern world, a force to inspire the best in people and bring nations closer together. He created the International Olympic Committee, which he chaired for thirty years. His hope and vision drove the Olympic movement forward through many difficulties and disappointments. His heart is buried beneath a memorial at Olympia itself.

Did you know?

An Irishman named John Pius Boland was studying at Oxford University when he first learned of the Athens Olympics from a fellow student, from Greece. This man arranged for Boland to enter the tennis singles, which he went on to win.

Summer Olympics

1896 – Athens, Greece
1900 – Paris, France
1904 – St Louis, USA
(1906 – Athens, Greece)
1908 – London, UK
1912 – Stockholm, Sweden
(1916 – Berlin, Germany*)
1920 – Antwerp, Belgium
1924 – Paris, France
1928 – Amsterdam, The Netherlands
1932 – Los Angeles, USA
1936 – Berlin, Germany
1940 – Tokyo, Japan; Helsinki, Finland*
1948 – London, UK
1952 – Helsinki, Finland
1956 – Melbourne, Australia (Equestrian events took place in Stockholm, Sweden)
1960 – Rome, Italy

1964 – Tokyo, Japan
1968 – Mexico City, Mexico
1972 – Munich, Germany
1976 – Montreal, Canada
1980 – Moscow, USSR
1984 – Los Angeles, USA
1988 – Seoul, South Korea
1992 – Barcelona, Spain
1996 – Atlanta, USA
2000 – Sydney, Australia

Winter Olympics

1924 – Chamonix, France
1928 – St Moritz, Switzerland
1932 – Lake Placid, USA
1936 – Garmisch–Partenkirchen, Germany
1940 – Sapporo, Japan; St Moritz, Switzerland; Garmisch–Partenkirchen, Germany*

1944 – Cortina D'Ampezzo, Italy*
1948 – St Moritz, Switzerland
1952 – Oslo, Norway
1956 – Cortina D'Ampezzo, Italy
1960 – Squaw Valley, USA
1964 – Innsbruck, Austria
1968 – Grenoble, France
1972 – Sapporo, Japan
1976 – Innsbruck, Austria
1980 – Lake Placid, USA
1984 – Sarajevo, Yugoslavia
1988 – Calgary, Canada
1992 – Albertville, France
1994 – Lillehammer, Norway
1998 – Nagano, Japan
2002 – Salt Lake City, USA

Games scheduled and re-scheduled but cancelled because of war

The First Modern Games

The first revived Olympics were held at Athens in 1896. The programme included many events that were quite unknown in the ancient Games, such as cycling, fencing, shooting and gymnastics. The Americans fielded the best-prepared team (of fourteen men) and won the most gold medals (eleven).

The Greeks, with the largest team (211), won by far the most medals overall (47). In many ways the contests were rather uneven and disorganized but the really important thing was that the Games had taken place. The big question was – would they take place again in four years' time?

The finish of the marathon, with Spyridon Louis being accompanied on his final lap of the stadium by Prince George of Greece.

Getting Organized 1900–1912

Chaos in France

The second Olympic Games were almost the last. They were to be held in Paris, which was de Coubertin's own home, but there were so many quarrels among the organizers that they could go only ahead as part of a World Exhibition. Baron de Coubertin himself was ignored. This resulted in confusion, with the events taking place over five months.

Some events were **amateur** contests open to all comers. Others were **professional** championships and some only had French contestants. A French team beat the Germans at rugby. The British won the polo and tennis. The Americans won the golf. None of these sports were to be part of later Games. Many of the competitors didn't even know they were taking part in the Olympics!

Even the organizers weren't sure which events were official and which weren't. An official report was only compiled twelve years later! The only really organized element was the American athletics team, whose supporters often made up half of all the spectators.

The 1900 marathon was run in mid-afternoon heat through the backstreets of Paris. Theato, the winner, competed for France. In fact, he was born in Luxembourg.

Stockholm 1912: the disciplined marching of the Swedish team, entering the purpose-built stadium, was a fine symbol of these well-organized games.

America Goes It Alone

The 1904 Games were held in St Louis as part of another World Exhibition. Again this led to great confusion. All events were called 'Olympic', but some were professional, some only for schoolboys and others just exhibition matches.

It was so expensive to cross the Atlantic that there were only half as many entrants as in Paris. Baron de Coubertin did not attend. Of the 625 contestants 533 were American and 41 were Canadian. The only British entrant was an Irishman who had just emigrated to the US. Not surprisingly Americans won almost every event.

Did you know?

Many events at the 1900 Olympics were disorganized. Some sprints were run downhill. The discus and hammer contests were held in a city park where the contestants kept hitting the trees. Swimming took place in a river with a strong current. Some timekeepers were placed where they couldn't even see when an event had started.

Greece Tries Again

In 1906 Greece organized another Games in a **refurbished** stadium at Athens. Although de Coubertin supported them, the International Olympic Committee refused to recognize these Games as official. However, after the disasters of 1900 and 1904, the success of these Games helped keep the Olympic idea alive.

Britain Shows How

For the first time in Olympic history, the 1908 Games – in London – were separately organized by experienced sports officials. Countries were limited to twelve competitors for each event. Winners were given gold medals.

Sweden Gets It Right

The 1912 Games, held in Stockholm, were excellently organized. The Swedes introduced electric timing-devices and a public address system. Gymnastics became a major sport. There was no confusion and no quarrels.

The 1916 Berlin Olympics never took place, because of World War 1, but Stockholm's success meant the Olympics survived.

The Golden Age of Athletics 1920–1936

Changing the Programme

Only four sports have been represented at every modern Olympics – men's athletics, men's gymnastics, men's fencing and men's swimming. In the years between the wars, several events which had been extremely popular – such as tug-of-war, cross-country running, rugby and tennis – were dropped. Basketball, canoeing, skiing, ice hockey and speed skating were admitted as sports. Athletics continued to hold centre stage in public attention.

European Hosts

The 1920 Olympics were held at Antwerp in war-torn Belgium, which was too poor even to produce an Official Report of the events. Defeated Germany and its allies were not allowed to enter. Finland, with a population of only 3 000 000, won as many athletics gold medals as the United States.

1920: Paavo Nurmi (on the right) running in the 5000 metres, on his way to gold.

The Classic Events

Track and field, swimming, gymnastics and fencing are the only sports to have been part of every Olympic Games. Other sports which soon won a permanent place in the programme include:

basketball (1936)	rowing (1900)
boxing (1904)	shooting (1900)
canoeing (1936)	soccer (1900)
cycling (1900)	weightlifting (1920)
equestrian (1900)	wrestling (1904)
(field) hockey (1908)	yachting (1920)

Jesse Owens, black hero of 1936, with a German friend Luz Long. Owens defied the Nazi ideal of white racial supremacy by winning four gold medals.

The 1924 Paris Games were spoiled by bad feeling between American athletes and their supporters, and the home crowd. The numbers of women competitors and women's events were greatly increased at Amsterdam (1928) and afterwards.

Did you know?

- Paavo Nurmi, the 'Flying Finn', used to run with a stop-watch in his hand to time himself. He won nine Olympic golds and three silvers and set 22 world records.

- When the British team won the water polo gold in 1920 they were attacked by the defeated Belgians while the host crowd rioted. During the soccer final the Czechs walked off and the match was awarded to the Belgians.

American Superstars

At Los Angeles (1932), eighteen year old American Mildred 'Babe' Didrikson won the 80 metres hurdles and javelin and came second in the high jump, setting a world record each time. Excelling in sports as various as baseball and billiards, 'Babe' Didrikson was in the All-American basketball team three times and went on to win seventeen major golf titles under her married name of Zaharias.

At the Berlin (1936) Games Germany's Nazi government was determined to prove the superiority of its 'racially pure' athletes, but was defeated by the astonishing performance of black American Jesse Owens. Owens won the 100 metres, 200 metres and long jump and won another gold in the 4 × 100 metres relay. He finished first in every one of his twelve heats or events.

The Global Games 1948-1968

Going Global

During this period the Games attracted more and more competitors from beyond Europe and North America, and were held outside those continents for the first time. When London hosted the Games for the second time (1948), the defeated Germany and Japan were not invited. Still, there were more competitors than ever before and the medals were more widely shared. In all, 42 countries had at least one competitor in the first six of at least one event. At Helsinki (1952) the USSR (now CIS) joined in, beginning a long rivalry with the USA. The number of competitors was close to 5000.

Further Means Fewer

Melbourne (1956) was the first city in the southern **hemisphere** to host the Games. The expense of travelling so far meant just over 3000 competitors took part, the smallest number since 1932. Also, the Dutch, Spanish and Swiss withdrew to protest against the invasion of Hungary by the USSR. Egypt, Iraq and Lebanon withdrew to protest against the Anglo–French invasion to seize the Suez canal. This sort of political **boycott** was to happen on an even bigger scale in future years.

The 1960 Rome Games saw the number of competing countries rise from 71 to 83. Abebe Bikila won the marathon barefoot, and was the first black African to win an Olympic gold.

Did you know?

At Helsinki, Czech runner Emil Zatopek won the 5000 metres and 10 000 metres – and then the marathon, which he had never run before. On the same day, Zatopek's wife, Dana, won the javelin. They also shared the same birthday.

1964: the Olympic torch was carried by a university student born in Hiroshima on the day the atom bomb was dropped, in 1945.

1968: Dick Fosbury winning the high jump, using his own technique, which came to be known as 'the Fosbury Flop'.

Asia and Altitude

The 1964 Tokyo Olympics, the first held in Asia, were a brilliant success. As a compliment to the host nation, judo became an Olympic sport. To the shock of the Japanese a Dutchman won the top title in judo. The other new sport was volleyball; the USSR won the men's event and Japan the women's. Bikila won the marathon again – five weeks after having his appendix out.

The 1968 Games in Mexico City were held against a background of fierce riots as students took advantage of the presence of the world's press to protest against their government.

There were protests from competing countries, too, about the **altitude** and the effect that the thin air might have on distance runners. The International Olympic Committee replied that the Games belonged to the world, not just nations at sea-level.

The **atmosphere** did strongly favour Kenyans, Ethiopians, Mexicans and others who had been able to train at high altitudes. Swimming and athletics led in setting new World and Olympic records, far above normal for one set of Games.

Problems with Politics 1972–1992

As the Olympics attracted ever more competitors, **prestige** and publicity, they also became a focus for political pressure.

Worldwide television broadcast the Games via satellite and brought these exciting sports into the world spotlight.

Tragedy at Munich

The 1972 Games were completely overshadowed by an attempt by Palestinian gunmen to kidnap Israeli athletes. Eleven Israelis and five terrorists were killed. After a memorial service and a one-day delay, the Games went on.

Four Boycotts

African nations led a boycott of the 1976 Montreal Games because a New Zealand rugby team had played in South Africa – which was banned from the Olympics for its **apartheid** policies. The International Olympic Committee had no control at all over rugby, but that didn't seem to matter. The USA led the boycott of the 1980 Moscow Olympics to protest against a Soviet invasion of Afghanistan. Not surprisingly, when the 1984 Olympics were hosted by Los Angeles, the USSR led a tit-for-tat boycott, supported by its communist allies, except Romania.

1988: the closing ceremony at Seoul.

1976: The Romanian gymnast Nadia Comaneci earned a perfect score of 10 at the Montreal Olympics.

Despite these problems the 1980 Games saw even more world records than 1976 had. The 1984 Games were attended by more nations than ever before. The 1988 Games held in Seoul, South Korea, were boycotted by its communist neighbour, North Korea, but only half a dozen other small countries supported them by staying away. For the 1988 Games, the Koreans gave a dazzling display of efficiency and hospitality.

Peace at Last?

The 1992 Barcelona Games had no great political problems but there were certainly major changes, reflecting major events in world politics since 1988. The break-up of the USSR meant that Russia and eleven of its neighbours competed as the 'Unified Team' but the Baltic states – Estonia, Latvia and Lithuania – competed in their own right. The break-up of Yugoslavia meant that Slovenia and Croatia became new Olympic nations, while athletes from Serbia, Montenegro and Macedonia were admitted as 'Independent Olympic Participants'. **Unification** made West and East Germany one single, mighty team. South Africa, free of apartheid, was welcomed back and Namibia came as another new nation. In all 169 nations took part – ten more than ever before.

Did you know?

Cuba, which had not sent a team to the Olympics since 1980, won 31 medals at Barcelona in 1992, coming fifth in the overall medals table.

The Winter Olympics

Scandinavians Supreme

There were figure-skating events at the London (1908) and Antwerp (1920) Games but no full-scale Winter Olympics until 1924, when they were held at Chamonix in France. The most important winter sports meeting until then had been held at Holmenkollen in Norway. Competitors from Scandinavia dominated the Winter Olympics for many years. In the post-war period competitors from the USSR and eastern Europe became a **formidable** new force.

Advertising and Expense

From the 1930s onwards the Winter Olympics were dogged by disputes over the amateur standing of skiers who got money and equipment from ski manufacturers. Avery Brundage, American President of the International Olympic Committee (1952–72), was angered by the way businesses cashed in on the Winter Olympics to promote skiing as a leisure and holiday pursuit. In 1972 Austrian skier Karl Schranz was expelled from the Games at Sapporo, Japan for allowing his name and pictures to be used in advertising.

The bob-sleigh events, which need very expensive runs to be built, have been criticized on the grounds that, to be part of the Olympics, a sport should be open to large numbers of people. In 1960 the American organizers of the Squaw Valley Games flatly refused to build a run because only nine countries wanted to enter teams.

Did you know?

- In the Winter Games, the biathlon events combine cross-country skiing and rifle shooting.

- Canada won the ice-hockey three times running, but in 1936 they were beaten by Britain – fielding a team of British-born Canadians!

- In 1980 American speed-skater Eric Heiden became the first person to win five golds at a single Winter Games.

Sonja Henie, who was only eleven when she first entered the Winter Olympics in 1924. She went on to win the gold medal three times and became a film star in the USA.

Who can be Host?

It was originally planned that the same country should host both Summer and Winter Olympics but only a few countries – such as the USA (1932) and Germany (1936) – have the right **climate** and geography to do both. Even then, the weather remains unpredictable. At Lake Placid in 1932 the American organizers had to bring in truckloads of snow from Canada to repair the cross-country tracks. Lake Placid has hosted the Games twice, as have St Moritz in Switzerland and Innsbruck in Austria.

Bob-sleigh

In 1928, the USA four-man bob-sleigh team, captained by 16-year old Billy Fiske, won the gold medal. Fiske led the team to gold again in 1932.

The 1988 Calgary Winter Olympics two-man bob-sleigh event included so many contestants from countries with little or no snow that they competed informally for their own 'Caribbean Cup', won by New Zealand who came in 20th overall. Mexico was represented in the four-man bob-sleigh by four brothers who were waiters in Dallas. The Jamaican team had financed its training by selling T-shirts and a reggae record.

Hosting the Games

Hosting the Olympics is a massive task but cities are prepared to spend huge sums just to be considered for the honour. Manchester, England failed in its bid to host the Games in AD2000 – despite a government pledge of £53 million to build new sports facilities. The Games were awarded to Sydney, Australia.

Cancellations

After the success of the first modern Olympics the Greek government campaigned – unsuccessfully – for Athens to become their permanent home. The 1908 Games were due to be held in Rome but the massive damage caused by the eruption of the volcano Vesuvius meant that Italy could not afford to the expense of the Games, which were hastily rescheduled in London. The 1916 games were awarded to Berlin but cancelled with the outbreak of World War 1. World War 2 meant that the 1940 and 1944 Games never took place.

1964: the Gymnasium Annexe being built, in Shibuya, for the Winter Olympics.

Winners and Losers

Financing the Games can be risky. Montreal estimated that the 1976 Games would cost $310 million (£195 million). In fact the final bill was nearly $1400 million (£880 million), which left the tax-payers of the city and the province of Quebec with huge debts to pay off for years. It was an awful warning. However, the cost of the Olympic stadium and Olympic Village was not a part of the total Olympic budget. Los Angeles, by contrast, managed to make a surplus of over $200 million (£126 million) thanks to sponsors like General Motors, who provided vehicles free, and Xerox, who loaned photo-copiers. And, at no cost to themselves, the people of Los Angeles gained a new velodrome and swimming pool, archery ranges, synthetic tracks and a sports medicine laboratory.

Time to Prepare

Antwerp (1920) and London (1948) both had less than two years to get ready for their Games, but nowadays there is a long lead-in. Seoul (1988) was notified that it had won in 1981. Barcelona (1992) was awarded the Games in 1986. For Barcelona, the task of organizing the biggest games to date was immense. Apart from providing suitable facilities for 257 events in 25 sports and accommodation for over 10 000 competitors and officials, there were also 15 000 journalists and broadcasters to be taken care of – not to mention two million spectators. To help them out the Organizing Committee and its staff of 5000 had to enlist the help of almost 10 000 volunteers.

Did you know?

- Security is strict for each Olympic Games. Baggage and equipment are checked electronically whenever anyone enters the Olympic Village. Competitors also have to wear an identity tag the whole time they are at the Games.

- Olympic gold medals are actually silver – covered with gold.

Did you know?

- Strict Australian animal health regulations meant that the *equestrian* events for the Melbourne Olympics took place in Stockholm!

- Alcohol was banned by law in the United States from 1920 to 1933. During the 1932 Los Angeles Olympics the French team successfully pleaded exemption on the grounds that wine was an essential part of their national diet.

Against the Odds

Olympic athletes aim to be the best. Over the years many have overcome extraordinary disadvantages of illness or poverty to reach the highest standard.

Ray Ewry

As a boy Ray Ewry (1873–1937) of Indiana caught **poliomyelitis** and was expected never to walk again. He began his career as a jumper in an effort to regain the use of his legs, concentrating on standing jumps – long, high and triple (hop, step and jump) – which did not involve a run-up. In the 1900, 1904 and 1908 Games he won ten golds in these three jumping events, all of which were later dropped from the official programme.

1900: Laurie and Reggie Doherty, winners of the men's doubles, were the first brothers to win an Olympic title.

Did you know?

- **Hungarian Karoly Takacs won shooting golds at the 1948 and 1952 Olympics – after losing his right hand in an accident and teaching himself to shoot left-handed.**

- **Don Thompson, British winner of the 50 000 metre walk in Rome (1960), trained himself for the hot climate by doing his exercises in a sealed bathroom crammed with home heaters and boiling kettles.**

Percy Williams

As a child Vancouver-born Percy Williams (1908–82) suffered from rheumatic fever, which left him with a damaged heart. At nineteen he hitch-hiked across Canada, from west to east, to take part in the Olympic trials, and was selected to go to Amsterdam where, against the fastest field ever assembled to date, he took gold in both the 100 and 200 metres. On his cross-country journey back as a winner he was presented with a gold watch, a silver tea service, a bronze statue, a sports car and enough money to pay for his entire college education.

Wilma Rudolph

Wilma Rudolph of Tennessee weighed only two kilograms when she was born in 1940, the seventeenth of nineteen children. At four she nearly died of pneumonia and scarlet fever, which paralysed her left leg until she was seven and forced her to wear a corrective shoe until she was eleven. Her potential as an athlete was spotted by a coach who saw her play basketball. At Rome she won the 100 metres and 200 metres and picked up a third gold as a member of the 4×100 metres relay team.

1960: Wilma Rudolph overcame childhood illness to become an Olympic gold star.

Discontinued sports

The following failed to become permanent additions to the Olympic programme. The years in brackets show when these were staged.

Cricket (1900: only Britain and France played. Britain won. Most of the French team were actually British.)

Croquet (1900: France won all six events.)

Golf (1900; 1904: 1900 included a women's nine-hole event in which Americans took the first three places.)

Jeu de Paume – 'Real Tennis' (1908)

Lacrosse (1904; 1908: Canada won both times.)

Motor boating (1908)

Polo (1900; 1908; 1920; 1924; 1936)

Racquets (1908)

Roque – a variety of croquet (1904)

Rugby (1900; 1908; 1920; 1924)

Tug-of-war (1900; 1904; 1908; 1912; 1920: teams of British policemen took all three top places in 1908.)

The Olympic Village

1932: the first Olympic Village was built for the Los Angeles Games.

The First Village

Paris in 1924 provided huts around the famous Colombes stadium, but it was Los Angeles in 1932 which created the first ever purpose-built 'Olympic Village'. Covering 250 **acres** on a hilltop only ten minutes from the Olympic stadium, it consisted of neatly spaced rows of two-room cottages and was complete with its own post office, hospital and police and fire stations. There were separate dining-rooms to take account of differing national tastes in food.

Making Do

Finding athletes somewhere to stay was a fairly chancy matter at the early Olympics. At Stockholm in 1912 the American team simply stayed on the liner which had brought them across the Atlantic. At Antwerp in 1920 competitors were housed in the city's schools, sleeping eight to a classroom. The British team organized evening dances on a school playground.

The Village was built to house the 1281 male competitors. The 127 women stayed in a hotel in Los Angeles. There were guards to keep the women out of the Village!

The 1936 Berlin Olympic Village was even larger and grander than the Los Angeles one, with brick-built cottages and no fewer than 38 different dining-halls. In 1948 war-torn London could only offer schools and former army and air-force camps. Athletes brought their own food and gave any surpluses to local hospitals. At Helsinki in 1952 the Communist countries insisted that their athletes live apart from the rest in their own separate village, near a Soviet army base.

Bigger and Better

As the scale of the Games has increased, Olympic Villages have become ever larger and more elaborate. One way of off-setting the cost has been to make Olympic preparations part of the host city's own development.

For the 1992 Games Barcelona built a new airport terminal and **marina**. They diverted a coastal railway line in order to clear an old run-down industrial area as the site for the Olympic Village at Parc de Mar Bella. The Village consisted of low-rise apartments for 15 000 people. Local people bought them to live in after the Olympics. They were sold before they had even been occupied by the athletes.

Atlanta Preparations

Atlanta's preparations involved the building of ten new sports venues, eight of them permanent, and Centennial Olympic Park in the heart of the city itself. The Olympic Village, needed to house 14 000 athletes and officials, included permanent new halls of residence to be taken over by Georgia Institute of Technology. Preparations also required the selection of 10 000 torch-bearers to carry the Olympic flame across America.

The stadium for the 1996 Olympic Games, under construction in Atlanta.

The Olympic Ceremonies

Past

In ancient Greece the Olympic Games lasted five days and at least half the time was taken up with processions of competitors and officials, victory parades, solemn **sacrifices** to the gods and feasts every evening. Both athletes and judges swore a sacred **oath** not to cheat. People who were at war called a **truce** during the Games. Winners received wreaths of olive leaves. Often the greatest poets wrote songs about their victories. Entertainment for the 40 000 spectators was provided by travelling acrobats, conjurors, dancers and musicians drawn to Olympia by the huge crowds.

Present

Traces of the ancient Olympics can be seen in the ceremonies of the modern Games, but new features have also been added over the years. The opening procession is always led by Greece, home of the ancient Games, with the host country coming last. Usually, the president or ruler of the host country formally declares the Games open and a flight of doves is released as a symbol of peace.

Medals are given to the winners of each event as it is decided, rather than all together at the end, as in ancient Greece. Finally there is a closing procession and a summons to the youth of the world to come together for another competition in four years' time.

THE IMPORTANT THING IN THE OLYMPIC GAMES IS NOT WINNING BUT TAKING PART. THE ESSENTIAL THING IN LIFE IS NOT CONQUERING BUT FIGHTING WELL.

BARON de COUBERTIN

New Features

At the 1920 Antwerp Games, for the first time, an athlete from the host country took an oath of fair play on behalf of all competitors and the Olympic flag was flown. The Olympic flame first blazed throughout the Games at Amsterdam in 1928. It was brought by a relay of runners from Olympia to Berlin in 1936. The playing of national anthems and raising of national flags at medal ceremonies has been criticized as contrary to the international spirit of the Olympics. Athletes are selected as members of national teams but are supposed to be competing as individuals.

With the coming of TV coverage the entertainment side of the opening ceremonies has become more and more spectacular, lasting for hours. Seoul in 1988 featured thousands of dancers and gymnasts. Barcelona in 1992 introduced world-famous opera singers. **Cultural** events, which were part of the ceremonies until 1948, are reintroduced in Atlanta in 1996.

1992: the Olympic torch being carried into the stadium at Barcelona.

Did you know?

The Olympic flag was designed by Baron de Coubertin, the founder of the modern Games. Its five interlinked rings are often thought to represent the five continents from which athletes come. However, the real significance is the colour of the rings, plus the white background. At least one of these colours is found in the flag of each country in the world.

Guarding the Olympic Ideal

Amateurs and Professionals

In the early days of the modern Games strict rules about amateurism made it hard for poor athletes to afford to train and compete. As time passed some nations began to help athletes indirectly. Communist governments gave them jobs in the army or as teachers but let them spend all their time on sport. In North America colleges gave athletics **scholarships** to promising stars who were students only in name.

In recent years the amateur ideal has almost disappeared. Professional boxers and baseball stars are still not allowed to compete in the Olympics, but tennis, baseball and soccer players are. Now that the amateur – professional issue is at last being settled, another problem of sporting fair play has taken its place. Desperate to gain every extra edge, some athletes have taken drugs (banned substances) to improve their performances.

A Hero Fallen

Ben Johnson of Canada competed at the 1988 Seoul Games, where he beat his long-time rival, American Carl Lewis, to take the 100 metres gold. Within hours, a test of a urine sample revealed that Johnson had been taking drugs to build up his strength. He was instantly disqualified and his medal was passed to Carl Lewis. Johnson was the 39th Olympic athlete to be disqualified since drugs-testing began in 1968, but he was the first of major importance since US swimmer Rick DeMont was disqualified at Munich in 1972.

Did you know?

If an athlete sets a national or world record, he or she is automatically tested for banned substances. Use of banned substances can lead to heavy penalties for athletes.

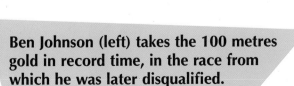

1912: Jim Thorpe winning the decathlon.

A Hero Humbled

The **decathlon** in the 1912 Stockholm Games was easily won by Native American Jim Thorpe (1888–1953). In those days the decathlon took place over three days. He also took the gold in the athletic **pentathlon**. But in 1913 it was discovered that Thorpe had once played minor league baseball as a professional. Although this had nothing to do with his athletic career, Olympic officials decided that Thorpe had broken their strict rules about amateurism, took away his medals and awarded them to the runners-up.

Despite a successful career in professional baseball and football, Thorpe died poor. Seventy years later, after a long campaign of protest, he was reinstated as a winner and his medals were presented to his family.

Did you know?

The founders of the modern Olympics thought that the ancient Greeks were pure amateurs who competed simply for the love of sport. In fact most were professionals and richly rewarded.

Ben Johnson (left) takes the 100 metres gold in record time, in the race from which he was later disqualified.

Screening the Games

Thanks to cinema and television, watching the Games is no longer limited to those who can actually visit the events in person.

Film

The earliest newsreel footage of the Olympics dates from 1912 and the first feature-length film from 1924. The four-hour film of the 1936 Games, made by the German director Leni Riefenstahl, took two years to edit and was praised as a masterpiece of cinema. In 1964 Japanese director Kon Ichikawa used 164 cameramen to make his film of the Tokyo Games.

Television

The Games were first televised in Berlin (1936), when events were relayed on a closed circuit to 25 local cinemas and halls.

Londoners were able to see events live on their own TV sets in 1948 – though only 80 000 homes had them. There were no cameras in the stadium at Melbourne (1956) because companies refused to pay for the right to film or broadcast.

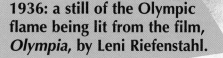

1936: a still of the Olympic flame being lit from the film, *Olympia*, by Leni Riefenstahl.

British figure-skaters Torvill and Dean, Olympic gold medal winners.

By 1960 this attitude had changed. American viewers were able to see the Squaw Valley Winter Olympics live on their own sets. The Rome Games were transmitted live throughout western Europe by a 'Eurovision' link-up between national broadcasting systems. The American CBS network paid $660 000 (£415 000) for the right to fly film to New York for prime-time showing. By 1964 the 'Telstar' communications satellite was in place and live events could be beamed from continent to continent.

Paying the Price

By 1968 the organizers of the Games were able to sell the American TV rights alone for $4.5 million (£2.8 million). By 1976 the price was $25 million (£15.7 million). The 1984 Los Angeles rights cost nine times as much.

Did you know?

- **There were 60 000 tickets available for the opening ceremony of the Tokyo Games – and 3 600 000 people applied for them.**

- **The proportion of Tokyo's population who watched at least part of the 1964 Games on TV was a staggering 99 per cent.**

The American ABC network paid $225 million (£142 million) – and still made a profit of $435 million (£274 million) from advertising. The 1992 Barcelona TV rights fetched over $500 million (£314 million) worldwide.

In return for these massive sums, Games organizers adjusted schedules to help the TV companies reach the largest possible audiences. The opening ceremony of the 1988 Calgary Winter Games was shifted from Wednesday to Saturday and the programme extended from twelve to sixteen days to cover three weekends. The top athletic events at Seoul were arranged so that Americans could see them at nine o'clock each evening in the East – which meant Germans had to stay up until two in the morning.

For the Record

Peak Performance in Paris

At the 1900 Games three roommates from the University of Pennsylvania – Irving Baxter, Walter Tewksbury and Alvin Kraenzlein – won fourteen medals altogether. Kranzlein, the pioneer of modern hurdling, won gold in the 100 metres hurdles, 200 metres hurdles, long jump and sixty metre dash.

The Greatest All-rounder?

Thirty-year-old Dutch mother of two Fanny Blankers-Koen left London in 1948 with golds in the 80 metres hurdles, 100 metres, 200 metres and 4 × 100 metres relay. Had she entered the long jump and high jump she would probably have won those, too, but Olympic rules restricted her to four events. In 1951 she set a new world record in the pentathlon.

Breakthroughs in Mexico

The 1968 Games saw two remarkable achievements in jumping events by American athletes. Twenty-year-old Dick Fosbury won gold in the high jump with an entirely new technique – taking off on the outside foot and going over the bar head first with his body facing upwards. It looked almost impossible – but now most leading jumpers use the 'Fosbury flop'. Bob Beamon produced what has been called the greatest single feat in athletics history – a long jump of 8.90 metres (29 feet 2.5 inches) – which advanced the world record by an amazing 55 cm (22 inches). Beamon's record stood until 1991.

1992: Chris Boardman on his way to winning a gold medal in the men's pursuit.

Perfection at Montreal

At the 1976 Games petite Romanian gymnast Nadia Comaneci became the first gymnast in Olympic history to be awarded a perfect score of ten – which she received six times in the course of the competition. She won two golds, a silver and a bronze, and at the 1980 Moscow Games won two more golds and two silvers.

Sensational Swimmers

American swimmer Johnny Weissmuller revolutionized the crawl and was the first person in history to swim 100 metres in under a minute. He won three golds at the 1924 Paris Games and two more in Amsterdam in 1928, as well as setting 28 world records. He went on to play Tarzan in twelve films.

Mark Spitz, another American swimmer, holds the record for most golds won at a single Games, collecting seven at Munich in 1972, all world-record performances. In the course of his career he set 27 world records.

Did you know?

Between them, father and son Swedish sharpshooters Oscar and Alfred Swahn won six golds, four silvers and five bronzes at the Games held between 1908 and 1924.

1968: Bob Beamon making his record-breaking long jump.

Glossary

acre unit of measuring land, about 4050 square metres

archaeologist an expert in the science of reconstructing past ways of life from physical remains, such as the ruins of buildings, tools, weapons, housewares, bones etc.

altitude height above sea-level

amateur a person in sport who does something without being paid for it

apartheid literally 'apartness'; policy followed by South African governments (1948–1991) which tried to separate the lives of black and white people; in practice this meant only white people got fair treatment in many fields, including sport

atmosphere conditions of the weather (especially the air) in a particular place or country

boycott refuse to have anything to do with an event, person or group

climate the type of weather a country usually has

cultural events which are more artistic than sporting, such as poetry, art and drama

decathlon contest involving ten events over two days; day 1 – 100 and 400 metres, long and high jump and shot put, day 2 – 110 metre hurdles, discus, pole vault, javelin and 1500 metres

discus heavy circular plate of metal or stone thrown as a test of strength

equestrian having to do with horse-riding

excavate systematically and carefully dig a site to reveal buried objects

exemption the right to be excused from something

formidable powerful and strong

hemisphere half of the world: the northern hemisphere is the part of the world north of the equator, and the southern hemisphere is south of the equator

javelin a throwing-spear; the minimum weight must be 800 grams (1 pound 12.25 ounces) and length 2.60 metres (8 feet 6.25 inches); it may be made of wood or metal

marina sheltered area of a seashore where boating and water sports can be carried out

oath a very solemn promise; breaking an oath can bring disgrace and punishment

pentathlon ancient Olympic athletic competition involving five events – running, jumping, discus, javelin and wrestling; if a clear winner emerged early on it was sometimes unnecessary to include the wrestling. Modern pentathlon involves running, swimming, pistol shooting, horseback riding and fencing

poliomyelitis infectious disease which can cause temporary or permanent paralysis by damaging the spinal cord

prestige good standing, being well thought of by others

professional a person who does an activity as a means of making their living from it

refurbished a building that is refurbished is repaired and modernized, to bring it up to a high standard

sacrifice an offering in honour of the gods, often involving the killing and burning of an animal; sacrifices could be made to ask a favour or to give thanks for one

scholarship payment or grant made to help a student to follow a course of training

technique way of doing something

truce a short break in a war, agreed by both sides, when they stop fighting

unification the bringing together of a country, such as Germany, which had been split after World War 2, with the eastern part controlled by the USSR

Index

Numbers in plain type (23) refer to the text; numbers in italic (13) refer to a caption.